W9-AUY-453

ISLANDS OF
SCOTLAND

Colin Baxter Photography, Grantown-on-Spey, Scotland

ISLANDS OF SCOTLAND

There are an almost uncountable myriad of islands scattered around Scotland's coast. They are so varied, evoke such different atmospheres, and offer such different experiences that it is almost impossible to sum them up as a single group.

Even within the main groups – from Arran in the south to the Inner and Outer Hebrides of the west, and from Orkney and Shetland in the north – the variety of landscape is too great to define them. Compare the soaring Paps of Jura with the gentle green landscape of neighbouring Islay, or the rolling peat of Lewis moorland with the rugged mountains of its conjoined neighbour, Harris; or some of the highest cliffs in Britain with the sandy beaches around Orkney and Shetland.

But there are threads which weave the islands together: the slower and gentler pace of life; the influence of an ancient Celtic culture which pervades language, identity and ancient monuments in the west; the seabirds and sea creatures from puffins to grey seals; and, of course, the famous island whiskies with their own distinctive flavours.

This collection grasps that almost undefinable weave of characteristics. It ranges across the ancient works of man on Iona to the startling beauty of the Atlantic beaches on the Outer Isles. It contrasts the cheerful colours of Tobermory's painted houses with the empty shell of the Village on St Kilda, and manages, at least in a small way, to capture something of the subtle nature of the islands of Scotland.

◄ BRODICK BAY AND GOAT FELL, ARRAN

So often described as 'Scotland in miniature', Arran is indeed clearly separated into Highland and Lowland by the Highland Boundary Fault which divides Scotland. The island is a geologist's paradise with granitic Goat Fell at 2868 ft (874 m) towering over the two very different landscapes; Devonian sandstones and schists form the rugged, mountainous northern half with its deeply indented coastline, and to the south gentler, moulded New Red Sandstone lies beneath rich rolling farmland.

SCALPSIE BAY, BUTE

On the south-western shore of this small island that nestles between Arran and the Cowal Peninsula, Scalpsie Bay lies at the edge of arable land made lush by the mild, wet climate. Bute is dominated by the town of Rothesay, with its 12th-century castle and a chapel dedicated to St Blane, who was born here in the 6th century.

GIGHA

The view north from Gigha's highest point, Creag Bhan. This tiny island bears the marks of centuries of human activity; cairns, standing stones, duns, a Viking burial place, medieval grave slabs and, more recent, the exotic gardens at Achamore House.

LOCH GRUINART, ISLAY ▶
Loch Gruinart, a Royal Society for the Protection of Birds sanctuary, is one of two main wintering sites for barnacle geese in the UK.

JURA AND THE SOUND OF JURA FROM KILMORY, ARGYLL

Distinctive from a distance the grey, quartzite peaks of the Paps of Jura soar above 'deer island'. So named by the Norse it still holds true with around 5000 red deer and just 200 people here. George Orwell wrote *1984* whilst living on Jura.

KILORAN BAY, COLONSAY

Once described as being 'as near to perfection as you are likely to get in this world',
the sweeping horseshoe of Kiloran Bay stands open to every mood of the great Atlantic.
Colonsay's coastline is gently scalloped with curvaceous sandy bays such as this.

IONA

In 563 when St Columba brought the teachings of Christianity to Scotland, he landed here on the island of Iona (left). The view he saw then across the Sound of Iona and the Ross of Mull to the Paps of Jura in the far distance, has changed little. The present Abbey, pictured here, is located on the same site where Columba founded his monastery.

In the centuries following Columba's death in 597 the island was invaded by Vikings on many occasions and the monastery destroyed and rebuilt several times. But symbols of those times survive. St Martin's Cross (right) with its serpentine and boss carving worn soft by centuries of weather, dates from the late 8th century. It represents the continuing strength of the Christian community on Iona after those three centuries of Norse depredation.

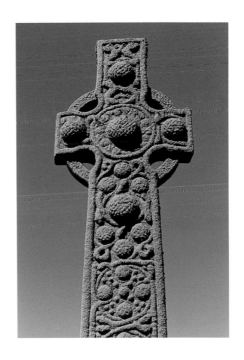

BEN MORE AND
DUART CASTLE, MULL

Sun-dappled or veiled in mist, the conical
summit of Ben More (3170 ft/966 m)
dominates the heart of Mull (left). For
seven centuries Duart Castle has stood
sentinel on the most easterly tip of the
island, home for some 300 years to the
MacLeans of Duart.

TOBERMORY, MULL

Founded in 1788 by the British Fisheries Society, the classic grid-plan form of Tobermory, curving and colourful, clings to the edge of the bay in which, it is said, a treasure-laden galleon of the Spanish Armada still lies. Whilst imprisoned on board in 1588, one of the MacLeans of Duart apparently blew up the powder magazine so sinking the vessel and sending its still elusive chests of gold to the bottom of Tobermory Harbour.

◄ BALEPHUIL BAY, TIREE

A typical dazzling bay in the south-west corner of the island. Fine, pale calcareous sands swathe the curving Tiree beaches, in contrast to the dark, acidic peat of the machair and the greys and browns of the intrusive Lewissian gneiss which underlies the entire island. Windblown across Tiree, the sands enabled the machair to develop into fertile, well-drained ground where grain can flourish and cattle thrive. These plentiful harvests gave the island its name, Tir-Iodh, 'the land of corn'.

ARINAGOUR, COLL

Picturesque Arinagour is the main township on Coll where half of the island's population of 150 now lives. With little shelter and no good harbours along its open coastline the islanders turned to farming, and more recently tourism, to make a living from the austerely beautiful landscape of beaches, dunes and machair.

▲ POLL NAM PARTAN, EIGG

For many, Eigg, meaning 'the notch' in Gaelic, is the most beautiful of the Scottish islands.

◀ CARN A' GHAILL, CANNA

Canna is an island of contrasts. Here on the southerly coast the land steps gently towards the sea from the summit of Carn a' Ghaill. To the north, sheer cliffs teem with seabirds.

Port-na-Caranean and Loch Scresort, Rum

Rum, Eigg, Muck and Canna form 'The Small Isles' which once gave a grudging living to 1600 people. When crofting could no longer sustain them, MacLean of Coll began clearing the islands in 1826 by shipping his tenants to Canada. Today, the ruins of Port-na-Caranean stand as a reminder of a once close-knit community.

ISLE OF SKYE

The sharp outline of Wiay and Ullinish Point in Loch Bracadale silhouetted against the western sky (above) is typical of much of Skye's north-western coastline. Towards the south of the island, the spectacular razor-edged peaks of the Black Cuillins (right) seem to rise directly from the water. Formed about 55 million years ago from gabbro, an igneous rock, they have gradually been eroded to form the present jagged skyline. So often draped in clouds, the island takes its name, *skuy*, from the Norse word for cloud.

THE SUMMER ISLES FROM THE AIR

HANDA ISLAND AND POINT OF STOER, SUTHERLAND

Handa Island is an important wildlife reserve managed by the Scottish Wildlife Trust.
Its sheer, Torridonian sandstone cliffs teem with large colonies of razorbills and guillemots
and an abundance of other seabirds. Its hue changing with the seasons, the moulded
surface of the island is carpeted with green, purple or russet moorland.

Castlebay, Barra

High on the conical summit of the Hill of Heaval a figure of the Madonna and Child watches over Castlebay where Kisimul Castle rises from the water. Romanticised in song, it was for centuries home to the infamous Macneils of Barra.

South Uist's Western Coast ▶

The gentle palette of the sweeping sands at Stilligarry stretches almost unbroken along the west coast of South Uist. This, the second largest island of the Outer Hebrides, is attached to Benbecula and then North Uist by linking causeways.

◄ THE WEST COAST OF HARRIS

Of all the Western Isles the name of this 'jagged island of peat and rock' is most widely spoken throughout the world. And Harris, famed for its tweeds, which weave together every colour in the island landscape, is formed from some of the oldest rocks in the world. Its mountainous landscape contrasts with the flat peat lands of its neighbour, Lewis. Ironically perhaps, this famous island name is not comfortable for Gaelic speakers for whom the letter 'h' should never begin a word.

CALANAIS STANDING STONES, LEWIS

Standing on the edge of the Atlantic, the ancient stones of Calanais were erected between 3000 BC and 1500 BC. Although analysed and examined in minute detail they cling to the mystery of their purpose. Lewis, meaning 'marshy', forms the northern two-thirds of the largest island of the Outer Hebrides with Harris being the southern part.

St Kilda

The deserted ruins of the Village on Hirta Island, St Kilda (left) commemorate a remarkably tenacious community of people who lived 110 miles (177 km) from mainland Scotland, often enduring extremes of hardship. They survived in almost complete isolation for centuries but the arrival of missionaries and other visitors brought education and disease which sealed the fate of the St Kildans. The last 35 islanders asked to be evacuated in 1930.

The stark silhouettes of Boreray, Stac an Armin and Stac Lee (right) mask the crowded commotion of the seabirds which breed on these awesome rocks. Now a World Heritage Site, St Kilda also has the world's largest gannetry, with some 50,000-60,000 pairs of birds.

ORKNEY ISLANDS

The ferry from the mainland to Stromness (left) passes the precipitous
Old Man of Hoy (above). This sandstone stack towers to some 450 ft (137 m).
In Stromness the atmospheric streets exude the harbour's history; the Hudson's Bay
Company, whaling, press-gangs, boat-building and more have all left their mark.

SHETLAND ISLANDS

Shetland's almost treeless landscape, such as at Weisdale Voe (above), is punctuated by sheer cliffs like these at Eshaness (right). Lying at the same latitude as southern Greenland, Shetland comprises many different islands. Though once economically dependent on fishing and farming, today it is better known for its North Sea oil industy.

Easdale Island, Argyll

In 1869 nine million slates were produced here,
the highest number since quarrying began in the 16th century.

Published in Great Britain in 2000 by Colin Baxter Photography Ltd,
Grantown-on-Spey, Moray PH26 3NA, Scotland

Text by Lorna Ewan

A CIP Catalogue record for this book is available from the British Library.

ISBN 1-84107-053-X   *Colin Baxter Gift Book Series*   Printed in Hong Kong

Page one photograph: **The Bass Rock, East Lothian**   Page two photograph: **Iona from Erraid, Ross of Mull**
Front cover photograph: **Iona beach and the Ross of Mull**   Back cover photograph: **Loch Maddy, North Uist**